Let's Get Moving™

The RUNNING Book

Jennifer Way

The Rosen Publishing Group's
PowerStart Press™
New York

For Lisa Dicus—you are the wind beneath my wings!

Published in 2004 by The Rosen Publishing Group, Inc.
29 East 21st Street, New York, NY 10010

First Edition

Book Design: Maria E. Melendez

Developmental Editor: Nancy Allison, Certified Movement Analyst, Registered Movement Educator

Photo Credits: All photos by Maura B. McConnell.

Library of Congress Cataloging-in-Publication Data

Way, Jennifer.
The running book / Jennifer Way.
    p. cm. — (Let's get moving)
Includes index.
Summary: Pictures and brief captions describe the movements involved in running.
ISBN 1-4042-2512-9 (lib. bdg.)
1. Running—Juvenile literature. [1. Running.] I. Title. II. Series.
QP310.R85 W39 2004
573.7'9—dc21
                                        2003006093

Manufactured in the United States of America

Contents

I run.

5

I run fast.

I run forward.

9

I run backward.

11

I run to the side.

13

I run up.

15

I run down.

I run in a curved line.

19

I run in a
zigzag line.

21

It is fun to run.

Words to Know

backward

curved

forward

zigzag

Index

Web Sites

Due to the changing nature of Internet links, PowerStart Press has developed an online list of Web sites related to the subject of this book. This site is updated regularly. Please use this link to access the list:
www.powerkidslinks.com/lgmov/run/